JEREM|

A MAN WITH A MESSAGE

TOLD BY CARINE MACKENZIE
ILLUSTRATIONS BY FRED APPS

Copyright © 2017 Carine Mackenzie
ISBN: 9781-7-8191-972-9
Published by Christian Focus Publications, Geanies House, Fearn,
Tain, Ross-shire, IV20 1TW, Scotland, U.K.
www.christianfocus.com
Printed in Singapore

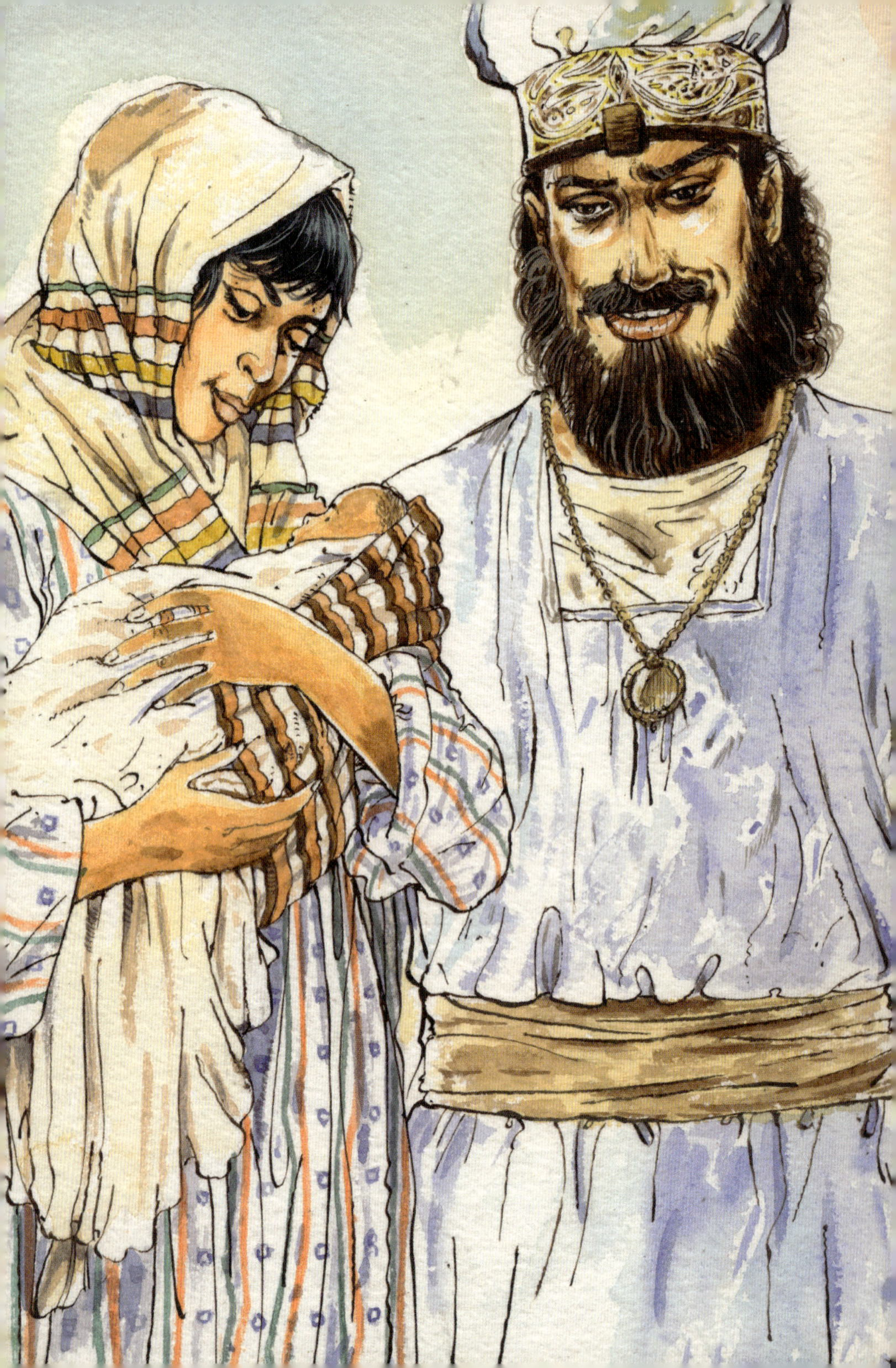

Jeremiah was born in Anathoth, a few miles from Jerusalem. His father was a priest there. Jeremiah was called by God to be a prophet – a man with a message from God to the people of Judah.

God had chosen Jeremiah for this important work even before he was born.

When Jeremiah heard God's call, he was very anxious. 'I don't know how to speak,' said Jeremiah, 'I am only a youth.'

'Don't say that,' replied God. 'You shall go where I send you. You shall speak what I tell you. I will be with you.'

When we feel anxious and troubled, we should tell God about it and trust in him and remember his promise to be with us always.

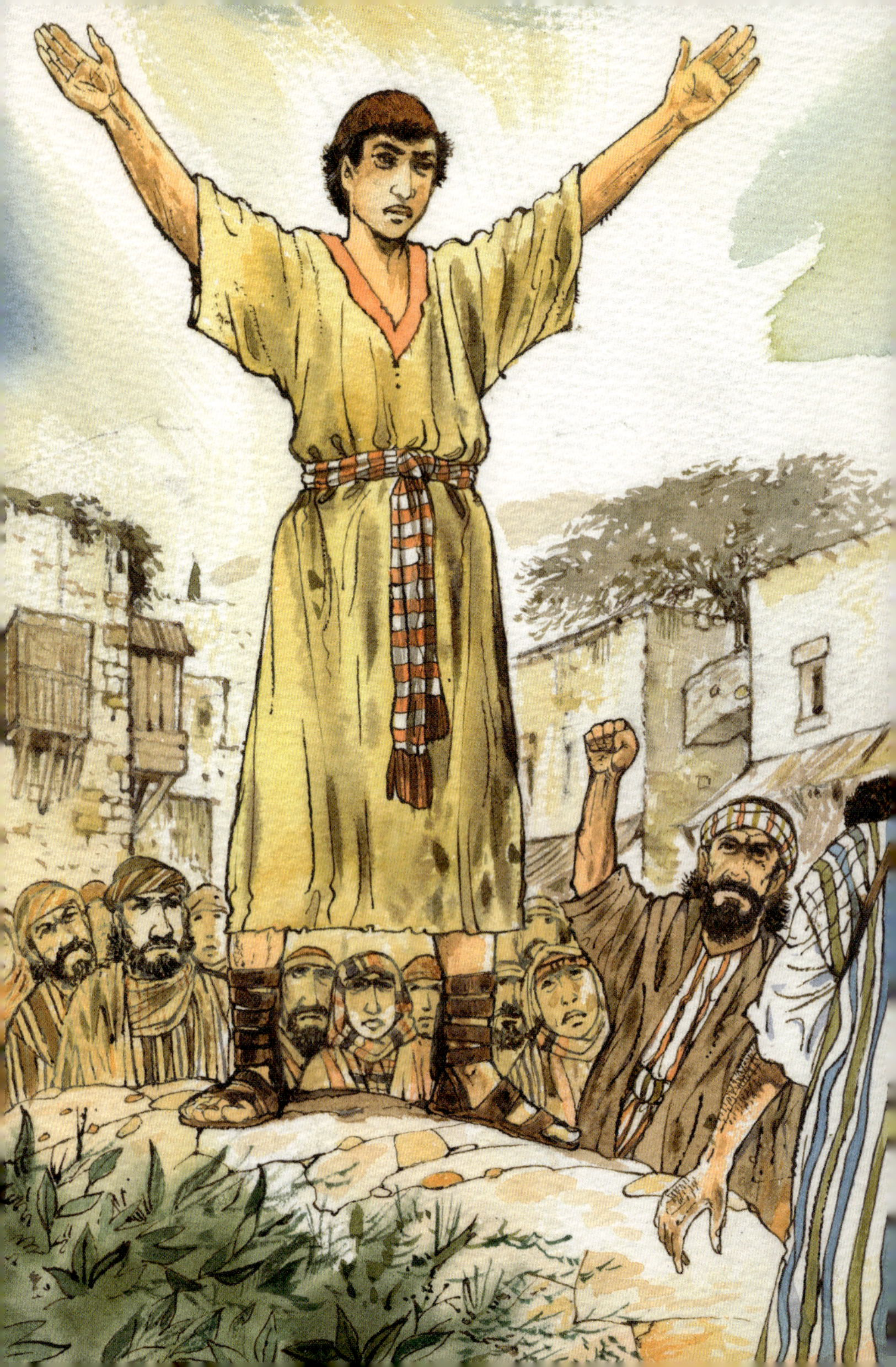

Jeremiah's message was not an easy one. Jeremiah felt great sorrow when he had to tell the people about God's judgement on their sin and rebellion. 'Man's heart is deceitful and desperately wicked,' he told them. Jeremiah wanted the people to trust in God and obey his Word.

Jeremiah was really sad about the state of his country. He cried many times over their lack of interest in God and his Word. He wept bitterly at the prospect of God's people being taken captive by an enemy nation.

God gave him strength and courage to speak out his unpopular message.

Jeremiah's life was really difficult. His message was not popular. People turned against him – even his own family. He was hated for speaking the truth. He complained to God, but God told him that things would only get worse.

God told Jeremiah to act out a parable. 'Go and buy a linen loincloth,' God said, 'and wear it closely round your waist. Don't even wash it.'

God spoke again, 'Take the loincloth and hide it in a cleft of a rock by the River Euphrates.' That was a long way off.

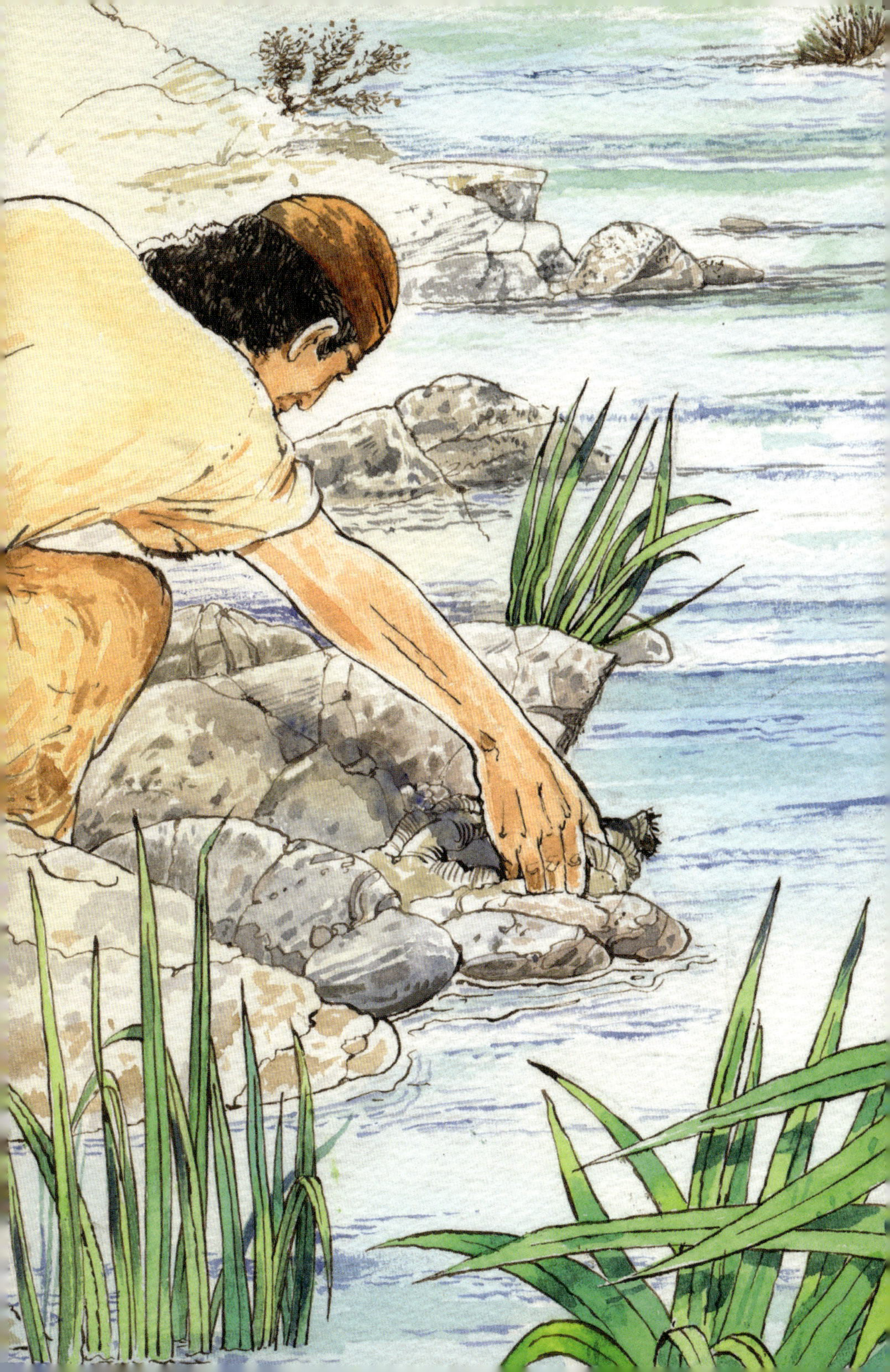

Many days later, God asked him to return and fetch the loincloth. It was now completely ruined and good for nothing.

God explained the meaning to Jeremiah. The people of Judah were his special possession – meant to be clean and pure and clinging closely to him. But instead they preferred a far-off heathen nation and so had become useless to God, spiritually rotten. Instead of showing God's grace in their lives, they dishonoured his name.

One day, God told Jeremiah to watch a potter at work at his wheel. When the potter noticed that his pot was not perfect, he took the lump of clay and re-worked it until it was right.

God is like the potter and the people like the clay. God can do whatever pleases him with his people. If they repent, God can forgive them. If they persist in sin, he will punish them. God was warning the people through Jeremiah that disaster was ahead, but there was still time to repent and to be made new.

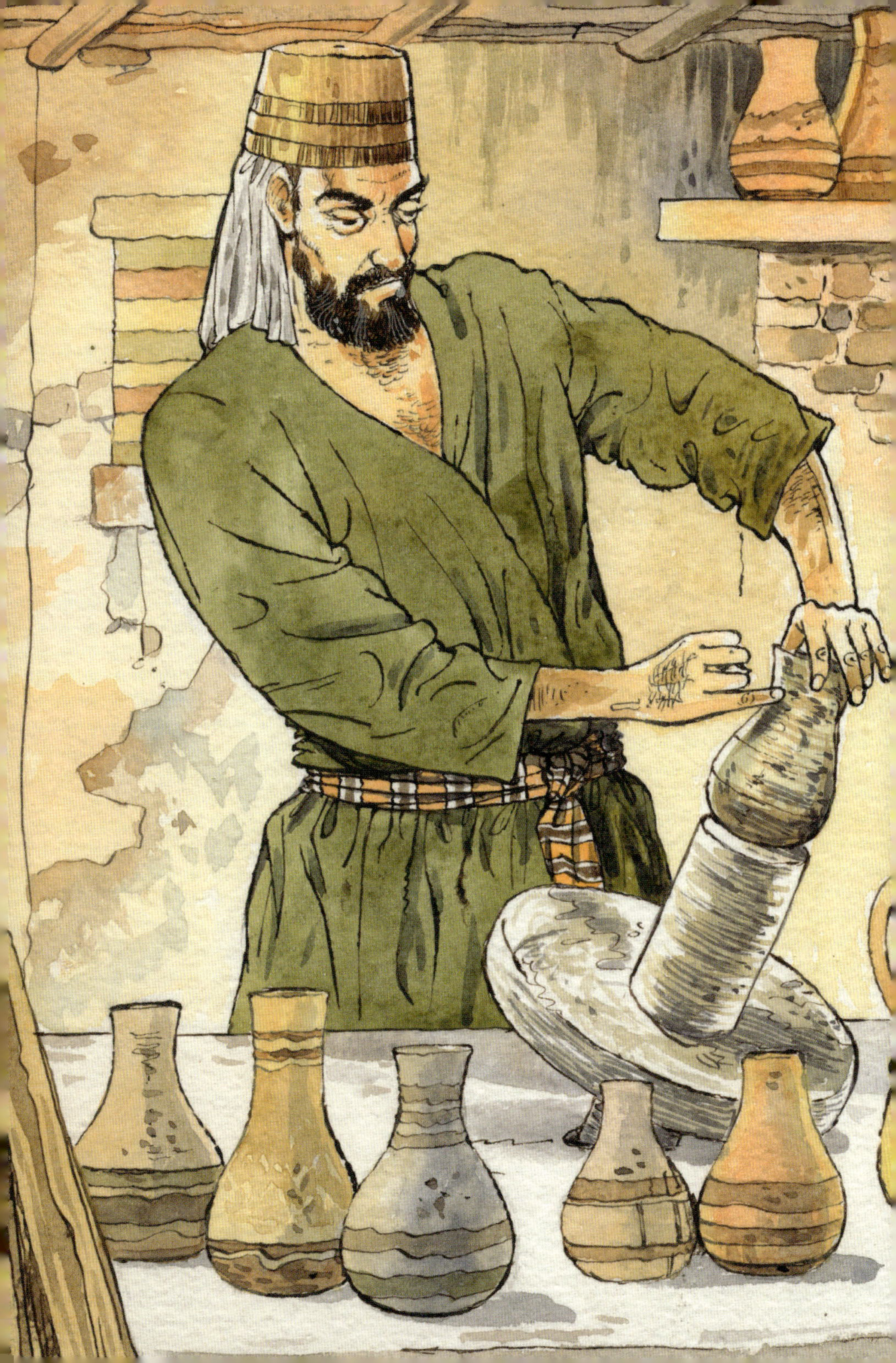

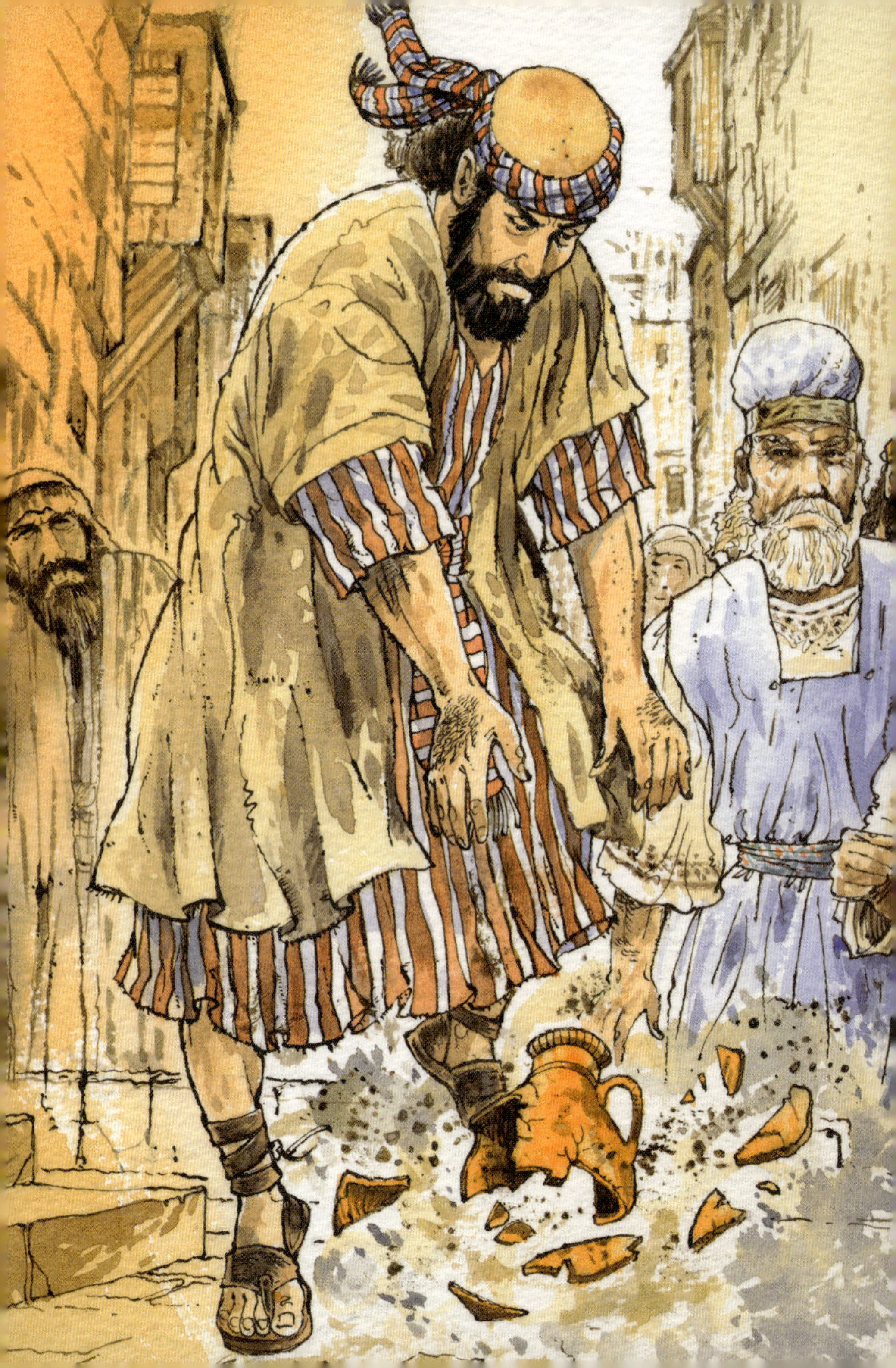

Jeremiah acted out another parable – he took a clay pot and in front of the elders and priests, he smashed the pot. This dramatic action showed the outcome when the people turned from God to idols – they would be beyond repair and useless to God.

When Pashhur the priest heard Jeremiah prophesying disaster for the nation, he was very angry. He beat Jeremiah and put him in the stocks – a wooden device which kept him from moving. But Jeremiah was as brave as ever and continued to tell God's message. He had to speak out because God's Word burned like a fire in his heart and he could not keep it in. Even when he felt sad and downcast, he still wanted to sing to the Lord and praise him for his kindness to the needy.

All through his difficulties, Jeremiah was sustained by the Word of God.

God's Word will sustain and help us too in any trouble or sadness.

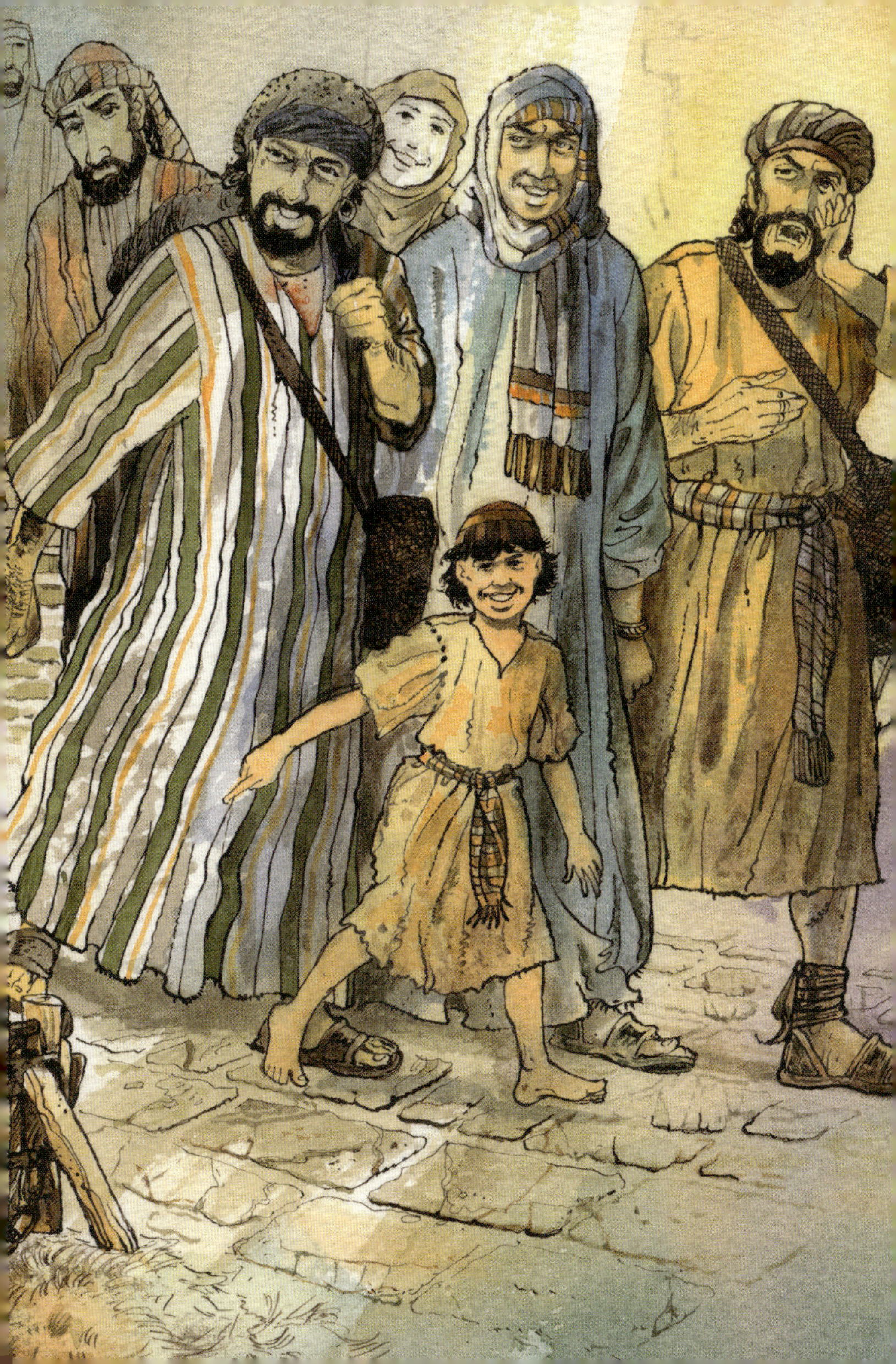

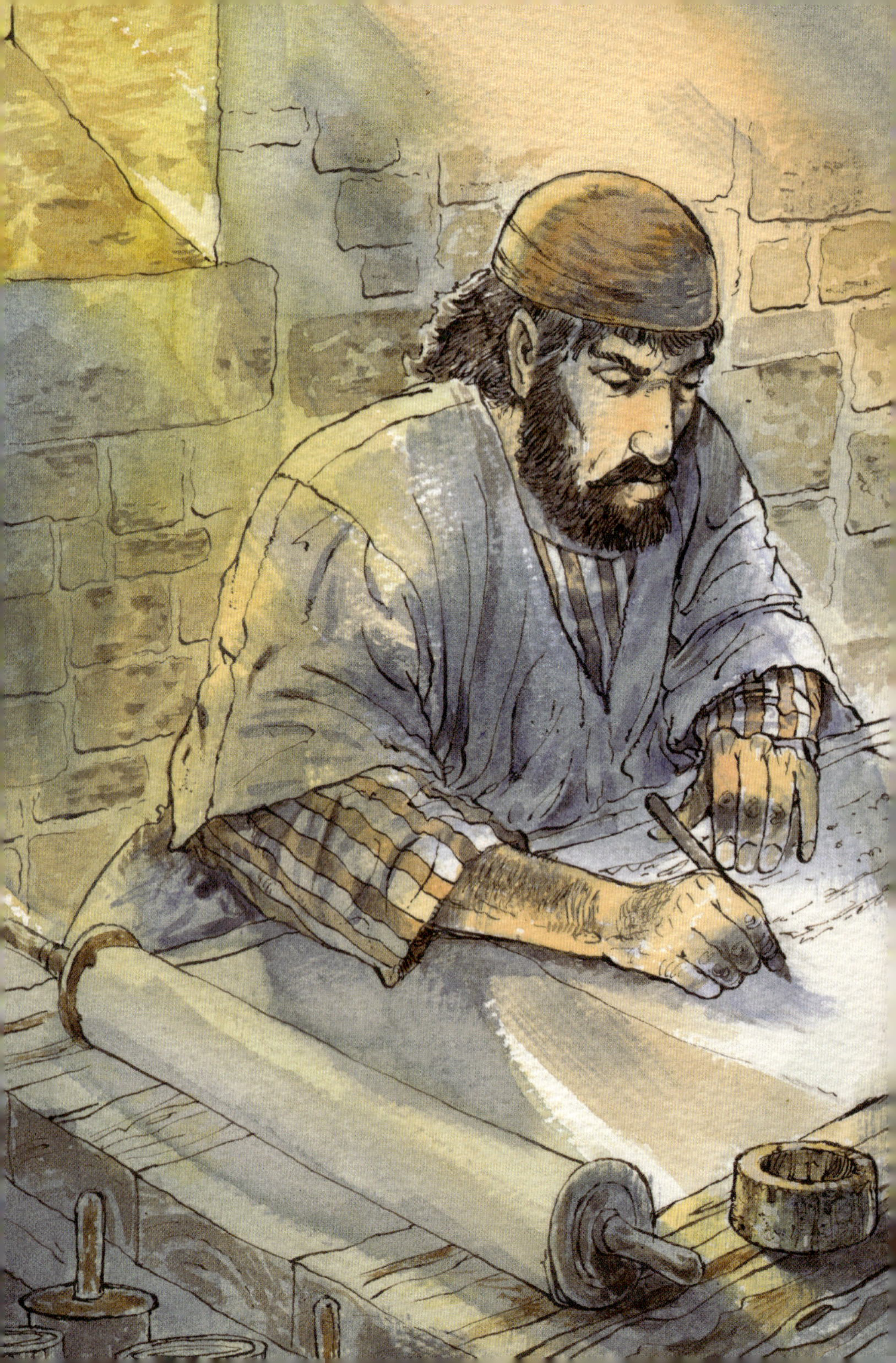

After the people of Judah were taken captive to Babylon by a foreign army, Jeremiah still gave them God's message. He wrote a letter of encouragement. 'Pray for the city of Babylon where you will be taken as a captive.' God promised that after seventy years in exile there, the nation would come back to Jerusalem. 'I have good plans for you,' God said. 'I will give you a future and a hope. If you seek me with all your heart, you will find me.'

In the middle of Jeremiah's prophecies of doom, he pointed to a time when God would send a righteous king – his special name would be 'The Lord our Righteousness'. The Lord Jesus Christ, God's Son, is this amazing Saviour that Jeremiah was referring to.

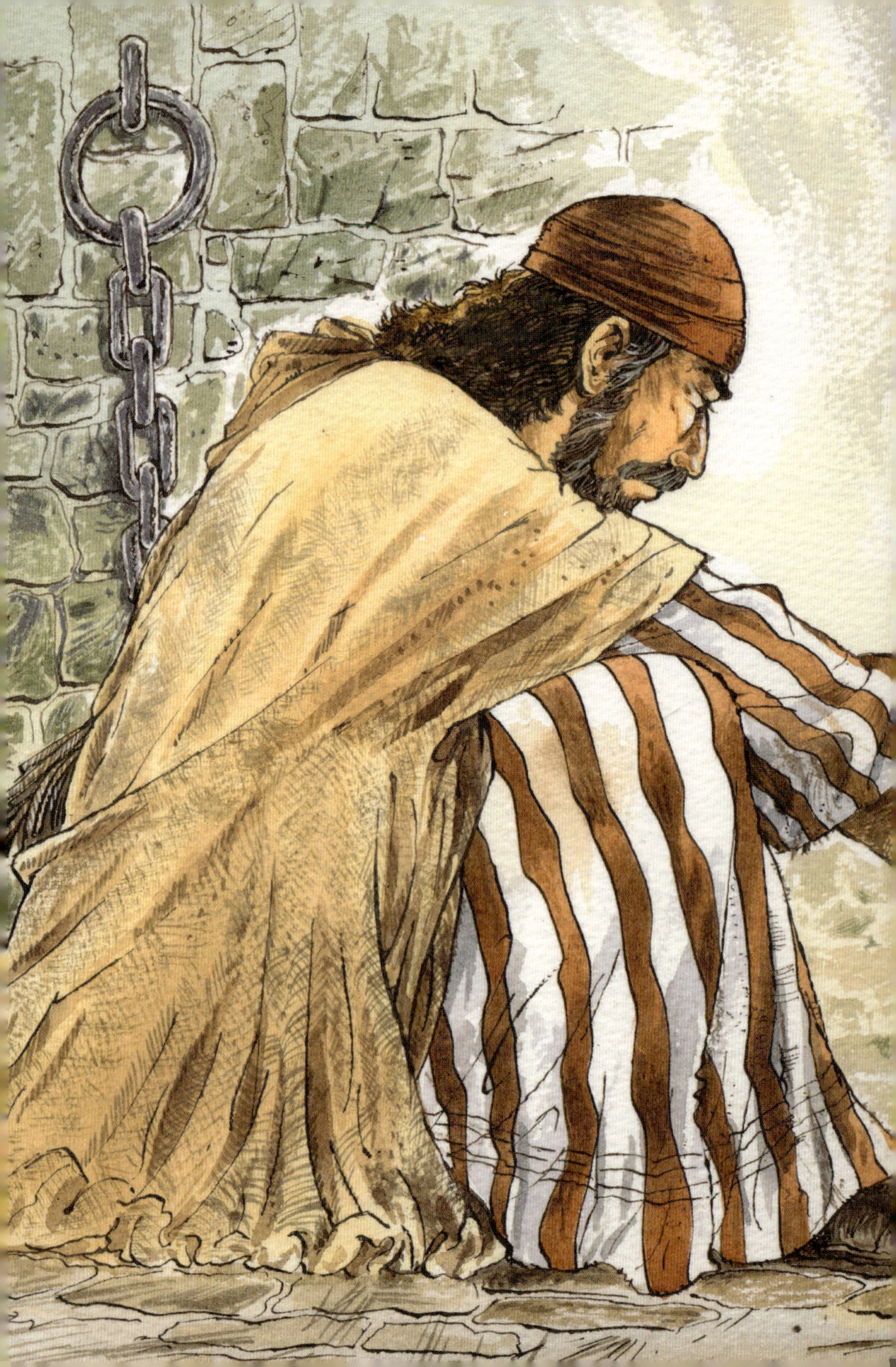

King Josiah supported Jeremiah, but his successor would not listen. Jeremiah was thrown into the dungeon below the palace. The Lord told Jeremiah to buy a field from his cousin in Anathoth, his home town. Why would he do that? The land was at war; there were enemies all round; Jeremiah was in prison. But this was God's plan. Jeremiah bought the field – the deeds were signed and sealed and put in a safe place. 'These papers will be valuable in the future,' God said. 'Some day people will again be buying and selling property.'

Nothing is too hard for the Lord. This gave hope and encouragement to Jeremiah.

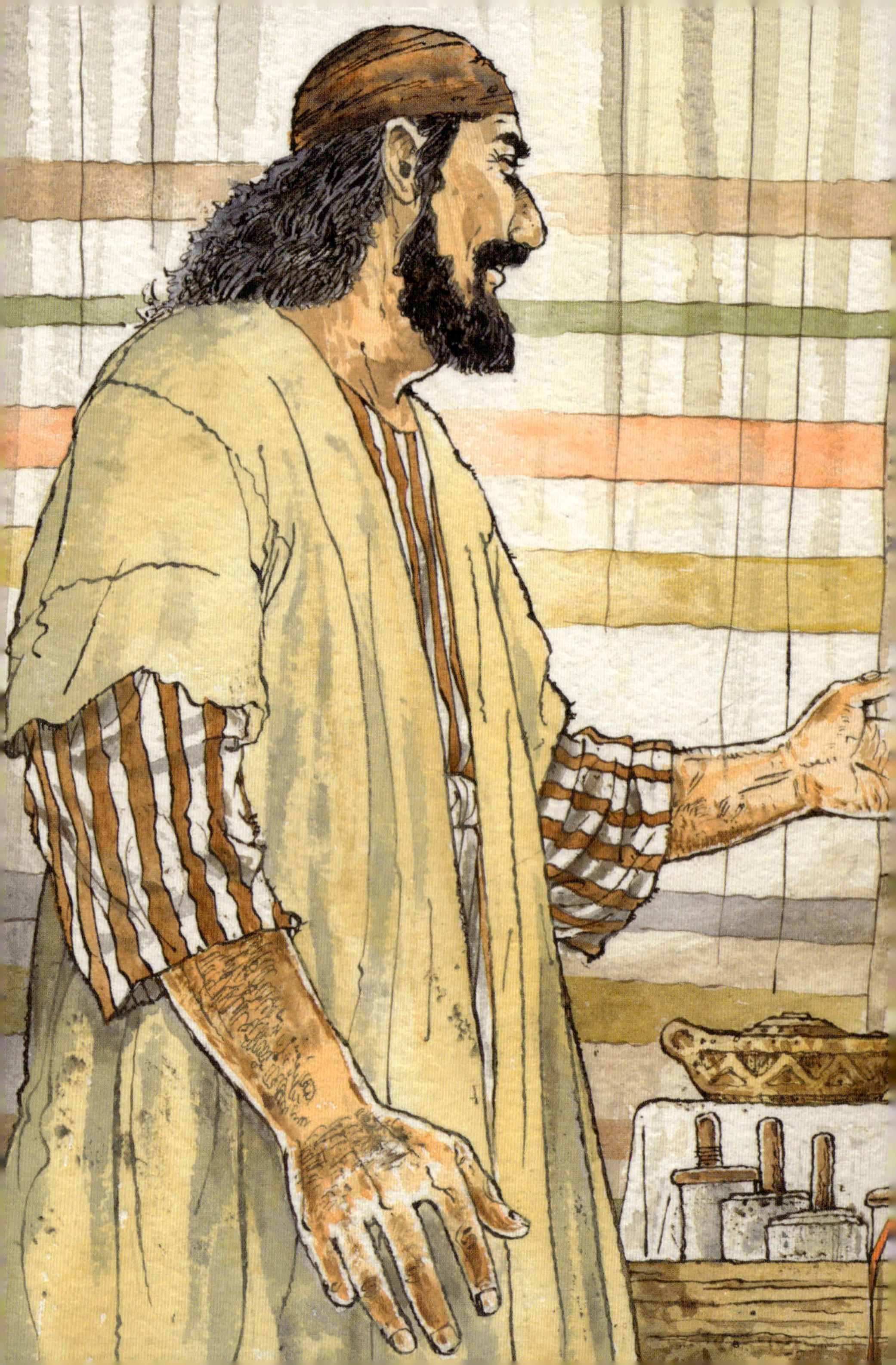

Jeremiah didn't have many friends. But one named Baruch, was his secretary. When Jeremiah was forbidden to preach, he dictated his sermons to Baruch, who wrote them down on a scroll.

'Read the scroll in the temple,' Jeremiah told Baruch, 'since I am a prisoner here. Perhaps the people will turn to the Lord before it is too late.'

After Baruch read the message in the temple, Micaiah reported to King Jehoiakim's officials. They wanted to hear the prophecies too. By the time they were finished, they were really frightened. 'We must tell the king,' they said.

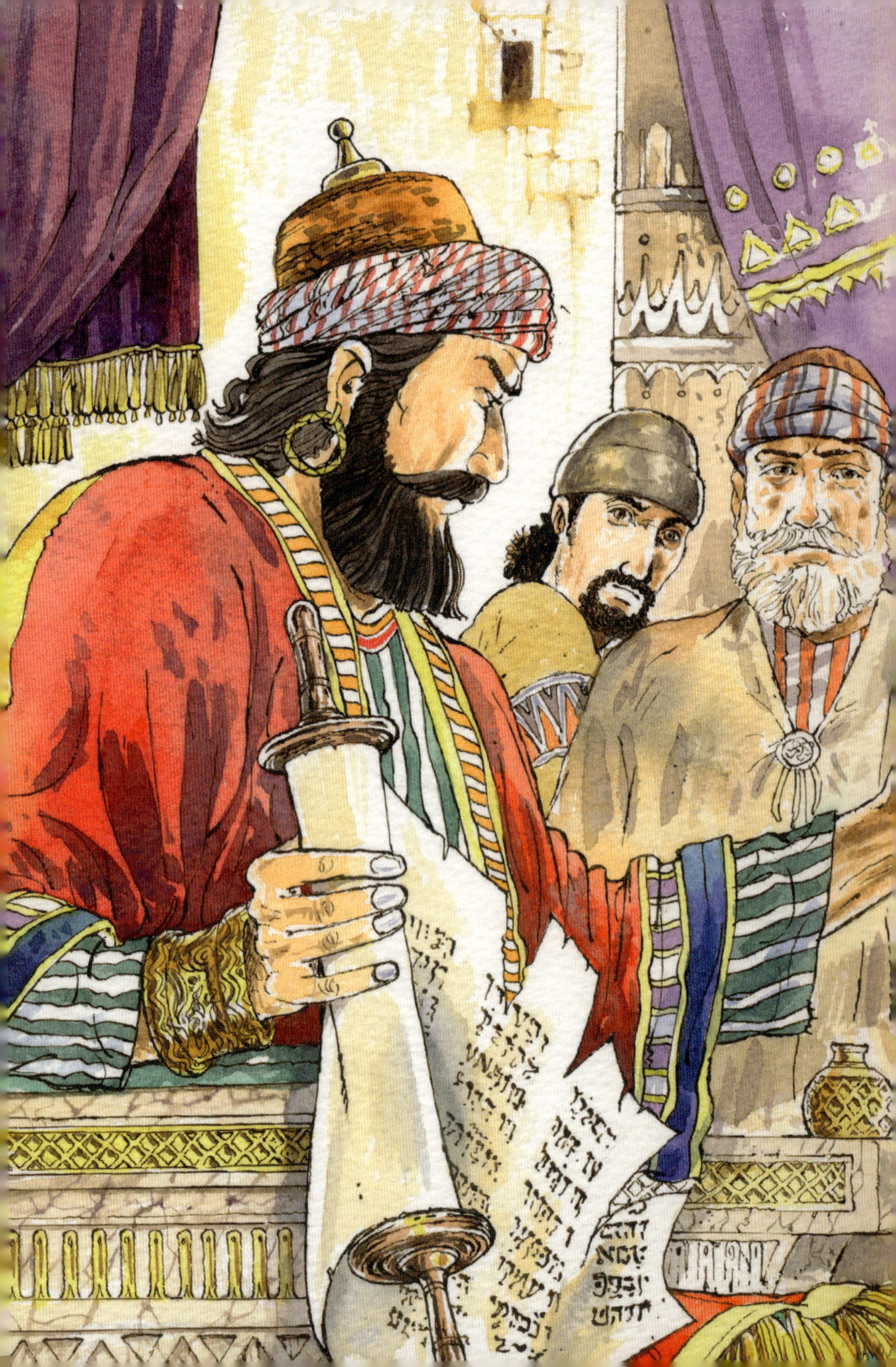

'You and Jeremiah hide,' the officials said to Baruch. They hid the scroll and went to tell the king.

The king was in his winter palace sitting in front of a fire, for the weather was cold.

Jehudi brought the scroll and started reading it to King Jehoiakim. After he had read three or four columns, the king took his penknife, cut off the section and threw it into the fire. Soon the whole scroll was destroyed.

The king wanted to arrest Jeremiah and Baruch, but the Lord hid them.

King Jehoiakim could not destroy God's Word. God told Jeremiah to get another scroll and write everything again just as he did before.

So Jeremiah dictated the message to Baruch again, but this time the Lord added a lot more.

The Word of God lasts forever. The king was able to burn the scroll, but he could not destroy the Word of God.

When Zedekiah became king, he did not listen to Jeremiah either.

One day when Jeremiah was trying to leave the city of Jerusalem, a sentry arrested him as a traitor. Jeremiah denied that strongly, but he was flogged and put into a dungeon for several days.

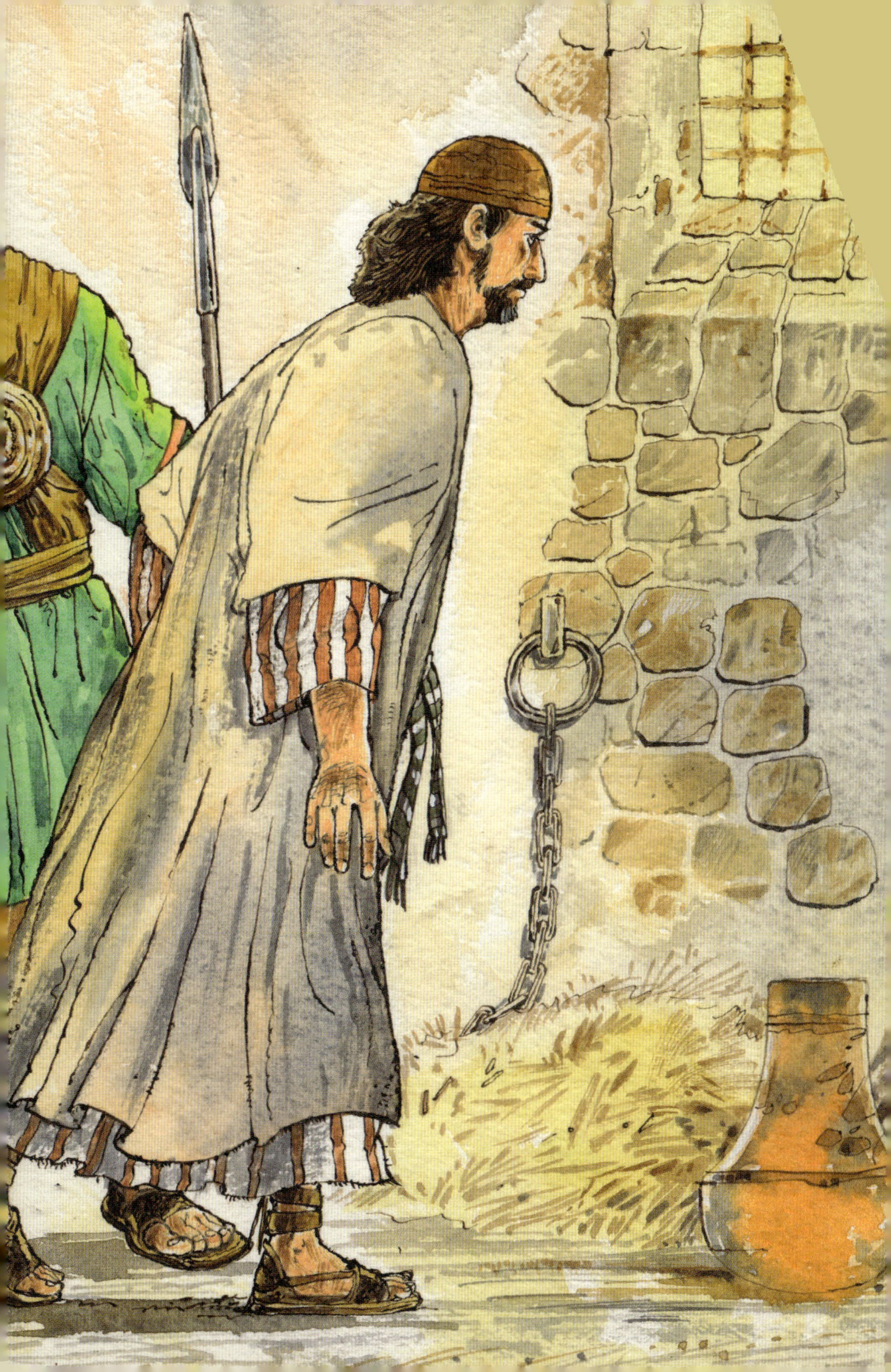

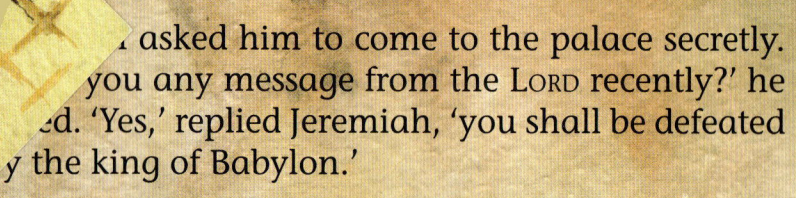

asked him to come to the palace secretly. you any message from the Lord recently?' he ...d. 'Yes,' replied Jeremiah, 'you shall be defeated y the king of Babylon.'

When Jeremiah complained about being put in a dungeon for no good reason, King Zedekiah relented a bit and allowed him to be put in the palace prison and be given a small amount of fresh bread every day. But not for long. Jeremiah's enemies stirred up complaints and Zedekiah gave in.

Jeremiah was lowered by ropes into an empty cistern in the prison yard. There was no water in it, but a thick layer of mud. Poor Jeremiah was most uncomfortable.

Ebedmelech, an Ethiopian, was an important official in the palace. He rushed to the king and pleaded for Jeremiah's life. 'He will die in that cistern!' So King Zedekiah allowed Ebedmelech to rescue Jeremiah. Ebedmelech went to the depot where used clothing was kept and found some old rags and discarded clothes. He lowered these down on ropes to Jeremiah in the cistern. 'Put these rags under your armpits to protect you from the ropes', shouted Ebedmelech. When Jeremiah was ready, Ebedmelech and thirty helpers pulled Jeremiah out of the pit. He returned to the palace prison.

Ebedmelech was rewarded for this brave and kind deed. God sent a message through Jeremiah to him, 'When I destroy the city, I will deliver you. I will preserve your life and keep you safe.'

After Jerusalem was captured, Jeremiah wrote some poems expressing his sadness at seeing hungry people and children suffering.

But he still trusted in God.

'God's compassion never fails,' he wrote. 'Great is his faithfulness. His loving kindness is new every morning.'

Jeremiah remembered that the Lord is good to all those who seek him. 'It is good to hope and wait quietly for the salvation of the Lord.'

The only way of salvation for us too is through the Lord Jesus Christ who died on the cross to save his people from their sins and give them eternal life.